Beastly
BUGS

Gareth Stevens
Publishing

Please visit our Web site www.garethstevens.com. For a free color catalog of all our high-quality books, call toll free 1-800-542-2595 or fax 1-877-542-2596.

Library of Congress Cataloging-in-Publication Data

Jackson, Tom, 1972-
 Beastly bugs / Tom Jackson.
    p. cm. – (Dangerous animals)
 Includes index.
 ISBN 978-1-4339-4035-4 (pbk.)
 ISBN 978-1-4339-4036-1 (6-pack)
 ISBN 978-1-4339-4034-7 (library binding)
1. Insects—Juvenile literature. I. Title.
 QL467.2.J35 2011
 595.7–dc22
                                    2010009085

Published in 2011 by
Gareth Stevens Publishing
111 East 14th Street, Suite 349
New York, NY 10003

© 2011 The Brown Reference Group Ltd.

For Gareth Stevens Publishing:
Art Direction: Haley Harasymiw
Editorial Direction: Kerri O'Donnell

For The Brown Reference Group Ltd:
Editorial Director: Lindsey Lowe
Managing Editor: Tim Harris
Editor: Tom Jackson
Children's Publisher: Anne O'Daly
Design Manager: David Poole
Designer: Supriya Sahai
Picture Manager: Sophie Mortimer
Production Director: Alastair Gourlay

Picture Credits:
Front Cover: Shutterstock: Craig Good.

FLPA: Hugh Lansdown 18; iStockphoto: 4, 9, 15, 20; Jupiter Images: Stockxpert 29c; Photolibrary Group:
Dennis Krunkel 3, 22-23; David Maitland/OSF 11b; Ken Preston Mafham 27r; Bryan Reynolds 29;
Science Photo Library: Gary Meszaros 13; David Scharf 25; Shutterstock: Florian Andronache 7;
John P. Ashmore 27; D Copy 19; Dainis Derics 6, 31; Cathy Keifer 10, 11; Kietr 26; D & K Kucharscy 4-5;
orionmystery@flickr 16, 17, 21; Sleepy Weasel Entertainment 15b; Jens Stolt 5t; Wong Hock Weng 29t.

All Artworks The Brown Reference Group Ltd.

Printed in the United States of America
1 2 3 4 5 6 7 8 9 12 11 10

CPSIA compliance information: Batch #CS10GS: For further information contact Gareth Stevens, New York, New York at 1-800-542-2595.

CONTENTS

Any words that appear in the text in **bold** are explained in the glossary.

WHAT IS A BUG?

Bugs are creepy little creatures that scuttle and wriggle around—often without us even knowing that they are there! Most bugs are harmless. Some do disgusting things, like eat dung or dead bodies—and a few can kill you.

There are many types of bugs. Some are wiggly worms or irritating ticks. But if you chose your yuckiest bug, the chances are it would be an **insect**. There are at least a million kinds of insects—probably many more. Insects include bugs like beetles, flies, fleas, and other little critters. Most insects stay away from people, but some work hard to sting and bite us.

Spineless!

Insects and other bugs are invertebrates. These are animals that do not have a backbone, or spine. Animals with backbones are vertebrates. They include fish, birds, and **mammals**—that means you, too!

Bugs do not have snapping jaws like us. Their mouths come in many shapes—like this tube-shaped weevil snout.

Bugs have bodies made of several sections: Spiders have two body parts, while worms can have dozens of segments. Insects have three sections—the head, **thorax** (the midbody), and **abdomen** at the rear. Insects also have six legs, and these are all attached to the thorax. Many insects have wings. Most have four, but some have just two wings. The wings are attached to the thorax, too. Some bugs can give a nasty bite, and a few can sting. Sharp **stingers** are used to pump poison into a victim—and it can hurt!

SCARAB BE

There are lots of different kinds of scarab beetles. They have rounded bodies and short legs, which make them some of the toughest bugs around. Scarabs are also known for eating a funny food—animals' dung!

Scarab beetles are busy bugs. They are often easy to see because they have bright and shiny bodies. **Male** scarab beetles may have horns for butting each other in fights. Many scarabs collect **dung**. They sniff it out with their **antennae**, roll it into balls, and lay their eggs in it. The baby scarabs eat the dung. Adults also eat flowers.

Sacred Beetle

The ancient Egyptians worshipped scarabs. They believed a giant scarab beetle called Khepri rolled the sun across the sky each day in th same way that real scarabs dung balls across the grou

ETLE

Huge horn

Abdomen

Leg

UP CLOSE

Some scarab beetles are massive. The male Hercules beetle is 7 in (18 cm) long and weighs 2 oz (57 g). That's more than a small bird. The beetle is also very strong: it can carry 850 times its own weight!

Common name:
Scarab beetle
Scientific name:
Scarabaeidae
Length: 0.2 in (5 mm) to 7 in (18cm)
Key features: round body, often shiny; large antennae
Diet: dung, leaves, roots, fruit, fungi, rotting meat, **pollen**, and **nectar**

FLEA

They may be almost too small to see, but fleas are the champion jumpers of the bug world. They can also spread killer diseases.

Fleas live on the bodies of mammals and birds. Fleas are small, so they can move through the hairs or feathers on an animal. Adult fleas only eat one thing—blood. They suck it through their **host's** skin. The fleas drop eggs onto the ground. The young fleas eat dust before jumping onto a large passing animal. It could be a cat or dog—or it could be you!

Thorax

No wings

Abdomen

Head

Leg

Antenna

UP CLOSE

About 700 years ago, a disease killed 75 million people. It was called bubonic plague, or the Black Death. The plague was spread by rat fleas. When fleas bit people, they passed the deadly plague on.

Common name:
flea
Scientific name:
Siphonaptera
Length: from about 0.04 in (1 mm) to 0.5 in (13 mm)
Key features: no wings; very flat body; legs used for jumping instead of walking
Diet: Adult feeds on blood; **larvae** feed on insects, dung, and plants

For the High Jump

Fleas have very strong back legs. That allows the tiny bugs to jump 150 times farther than the length of their body and 80 times their height. If a flea were the size of a person, it could leap over a building!

MANTIS

The mantis is a deadly hunter. It stands totally still and waits for **prey** to pass—and then grabs its victims with its spiked legs.

Mantises eat almost anything small enough to catch. Their large eyes scan for victims, and their head can swivel in all directions. Mantises use their long, folded legs to grip the prey as they eat their victims alive. A **female** mantis makes a nest of dried **foam** for her eggs. Each egg has its own room in the nest. Baby mantises are called **nymphs** and look like small versions of their parents—but without any wings.

UP CLOSE

One kind of mantis is called a praying mantis. The way it holds its front legs looks like it is praying! Mantises can hold prey with one front leg and grab hold of the next victim with the other.

Wings

Front legs

Thorax

Abdomen

Dangerous Date

A male mantis needs to be careful when it mates: the female might bite his head off! This happens when the female is so hungry that she forgets that her mate is not food.

Common name: mantis

Scientific name: Mantodea

Length: 0.4 in (1 cm) to 6 in (15 cm)

Key features: large eyes set widely apart; thin antennae; long thorax and leathery wings

Diet: insects and spiders, sometimes small lizards

CARRION

These are little bugs with big appetites. The adult beetles bury the bodies of dead animals, and then their baby grubs eat the corpse in its grave!

Carrion is the name for the meat of dead animals. Carrion beetles search for the fresh body of a mouse or bird. The body provides food for the adults and their **grubs**. Some carrion beetles bury their food quickly, before other bugs can lay their eggs on it. Others leave it to rot and slowly feast on the flesh.

UP CLOSE

Like all types of beetles, carrion beetles have two sets of wings. However, the front wings are not used for flying. Instead, they form hard wing cases called elytra. These protect the delicate hind wings.

BEETLE

Tasty Maggots

Some carrion beetles do not like fresh carrion. Instead, they wait for the body to be filled with **maggots**. Yuck! The beetle grubs then feast on these wriggly tidbits.

FACT

The American burying beetle works hard to raise its young. After burying a dead animal's body, the bug strips the skin from it, making a ball of flesh. When grubs hatch, the female feeds the babies until they are big enough to do it themselves.

Common name: carrion beetle, or sexton beetle

Scientific name: Silphidae

Length: 0.05 in (1.3 mm) to 1.6 in (4 cm)

Key features: usually dark with red or orange markings; body is flat; antennae are club-shaped

Diet: dead animals, such as mice, and snails, slugs, and dead plants

COCKROACH

This bug is famous for being yucky. Where people have left a mess, you soon find cockroaches! However, most cockroaches never see a person. Only 25 of the 4,000 kinds of cockroaches live near people.

Antenna

Thorax

Cockroaches eat almost anything, including the food that people leave lying around. The bugs have a flattened body so they can squeeze into small spaces, such as cracks in walls or under bark. Many cockroaches eat dead wood. The mother cockroach lays eggs in the rotten wood. When the eggs hatch, the mother feeds her babies on bug milk.

Wings

Leg

UP CLOSE

Cockroaches generally come out to feed at night. They have very long, thin antennae. The roaches use them to feel their way in the dark and to search for food.

Common name:
cockroach, or woodroach
Scientific name:
Blattodea
Length: 0.15 in (4 mm) to 4.8 in (12 cm)
Key features: flattened body; long antennae; thick forewings
Diet: will eat almost anything

Angry Hisses

Male cockroaches fight with each other over females. They try to push other males away. Males hiss loudly in battle, so fights can be very noisy!

WEEVIL

These bugs can cause big problems. They ruin stores of food and damage our crops. Weevils eat seeds and roots and also drill into plants and lay eggs inside.

Weevils live just about everywhere on Earth, including snow-covered islands near the South Pole and on high mountains. Some weevils are brightly colored and can be seen feasting on plants. Many others stay out of sight, buried in the soil.

FACT

There are more types of weevils than any other group of animal. Scientists have counted 50,000 species so far, but there are probably many thousands more.

Hairy body

Head

Antenna

Mouth

Leg

A Long Face

Weevils look like they have long noses, like an elephant's trunk. In fact, the bug's mouth is at the tip of the long face. The antennae grow from the sides of the snout.

Common name:
weevil, or snout beetle
Scientific name:
Curculionidae
Length: 0.04 in (1 mm) to 3 in (7.5 cm)
Key features: long snout curves downward; body often appears hairy
Diet: pollen, leaves, insect eggs, roots, fruits

LEECH

There are few other bugs as disgusting as a leech. These wiggly worms can drink your blood for hours. Many people never even know it's happening!

Leeches are distant relatives of earthworms. Leeches only live in wet places. Many of them live in the ocean or in ponds, where they prey on fish or eat insects. On land, leeches live mostly in steamy jungles. The largest leech in the world lives in the Amazon rain forest. It grows to 20 in (50 cm) long and stretches even longer as it reaches to grab a victim.

FACT

A leech bites the skin and then drinks the blood that flows out. Chemicals in the leech's spit stop the blood from clotting into a scab. The cut will bleed for hours even after the leech is full and falls off.

Flattened
body

Segment

Sucker

UP CLOSE

Leeches have flattened bodies made up of 34 segments. They have suckers at both ends of the body. Leeches stand on their tail, waving their head around. When an animal comes close, the leech grabs hold.

Medical Leech

Doctors use leeches to help heal deep cuts. The leeches are allowed to suck the blood through the sore area. They stop damaging clots from forming, so the wound heals faster.

Common name:
leech
Scientific name:
Hirudinea
Length: 0.4 in (1 cm) to 20 in (50 cm)
Key features: normally dark brown or black but also gray or green; long, flattened body with suckers on the head and tail; grows large and bloated after feeding
Diet: blood, insects, dead bodies

FLESH FLY

As you might have guessed, flesh flies are meat-eating bugs. Their maggots eat the flesh of dead animals—and even some that are still alive!

A female flesh fly lays her eggs inside dead animals or in deep cuts in living animals. When the maggots hatch, they have plenty of good food! The maggots spit stomach juices onto the food, which turns it into liquid. The baby bugs then suck up the fleshy juice. A few flesh flies invade bee or wasp nests. Their maggots feast on the honey and other foods stored inside.

Common name:
flesh fly
Scientific name:
Sarcophagidae
Length: 0.08 in (2 mm) to
0.5 in (13 mm)
Key features: gray body; striped thorax; red eyes; short antennae
Diet: adults eat nectar from flowers and plant juices; the maggots eat insects, dung, and rotting flesh

Singing Supper

Some female flesh flies listen for the songs of another bug, the male cicada. The flesh fly tracks him down and lays her eggs inside the cicada's body. He makes a tasty meal for the maggots when they hatch!

UP CLOSE

Flesh flies usually have large red eyes and stripes on the thorax. The adult flies eat nectar and other plant juices. Only the wormlike maggots feast on flesh.

Striped thorax

Antenna

Leg

Wing

BEDBUG

You can't see them, but bedbugs could be lurking in your house. They stay hidden during the day, but may come out at bedtime to suck your blood!

UP CLOSE

A bedbug bites with a long rostrum (pink in this photo) on the tip of its head. The rostrum's sharp tip sticks into the skin. Then blood is sucked up through it.

Bedbugs live inside houses. During the day, they squeeze into cracks in walls and the folds of cloth. At night, they hunt for blood. There are two kinds of bedbugs that feed on humans. Their bites itch but are not dangerous. In the wild, most bedbugs hide in caves and feed on birds and bats.

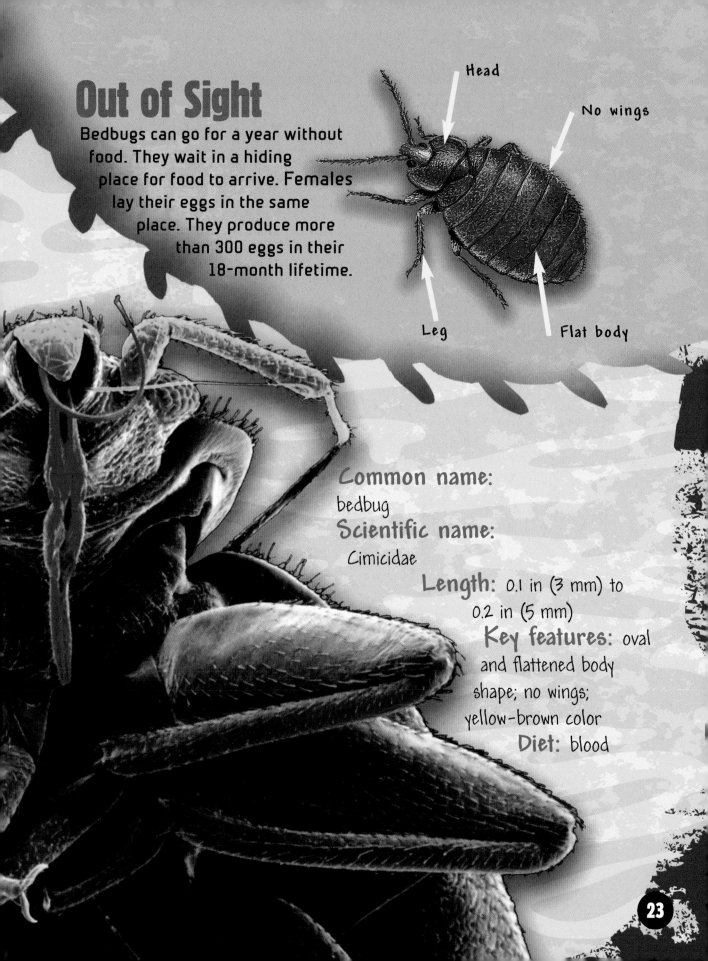

Out of Sight

Bedbugs can go for a year without food. They wait in a hiding place for food to arrive. Females lay their eggs in the same place. They produce more than 300 eggs in their 18-month lifetime.

Head

No wings

Leg

Flat body

Common name: bedbug

Scientific name: Cimicidae

Length: 0.1 in (3 mm) to 0.2 in (5 mm)

Key features: oval and flattened body shape; no wings; yellow-brown color

Diet: blood

HEAD LOUSE

It is hard not to feel an itch when you think about head lice. These little bugs live only in human hair and they love to suck the blood from your head!

Head lice hang onto hairs with their claws and attach their eggs to them, too. The young lice climb onto the head and neck and suck blood through the skin. Adult lice have no wings and cannot jump. They spread when people touch their heads together.

FACT

Washing your hair will not get rid of lice. The lice can close up their breathing holes so they will not drown in the bath. Special hairsprays or shampoos are used to kill the bugs.

Leg

Head

No wings

Abdomen

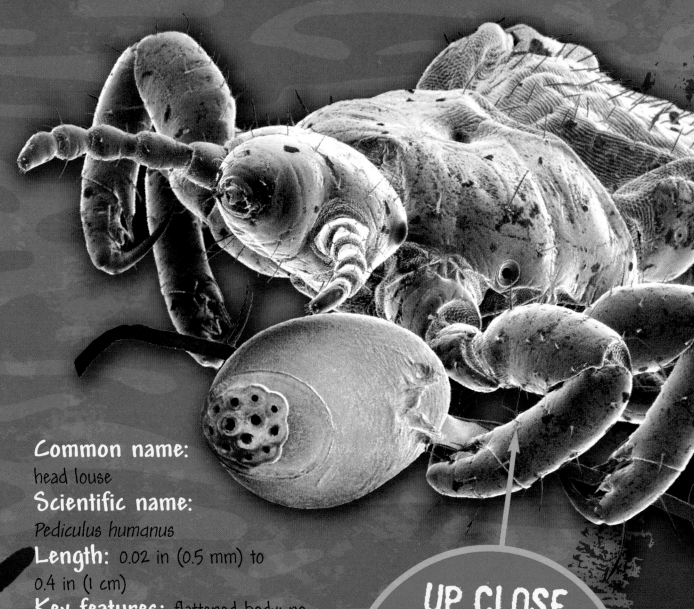

Common name:
head louse
Scientific name:
Pediculus humanus
Length: 0.02 in (0.5 mm) to
0.4 in (1 cm)
Key features: flattened body; no
wings; short antennae; sucking
mouthparts
Diet: human blood

UP CLOSE

Head lice are very small
insects. They are about the
size of a sesame seed. Their
bodies are light brown, but
turn red after a meal of
blood! Lice eggs are even
smaller and are
called nits.

Sickness Bug

Human body lice pass on more
diseases than most other bugs.
They spread typhus and trench
fever, which can kill people.

SOCIAL WA

These striped bugs work together to build a large nest. Thousands of them can crowd into a nest, but watch out—the wasps may sting you if you get too close.

Social wasps are easy to spot because they have striped bodies. Most are females. Only a few males hatch each year. The males do not have stingers and die after they mate with a queen. The queen is the top wasp in the nest. The other wasps are workers. They hunt for insects to feed the queen's young. The wasps slice up prey before bringing it home.

Common name:
social wasp, or yellowjacket
Scientific name:
Vespidae
Length: 0.2 in (5 mm) to 1.4 in (3.5 cm)
Key features: black and yellow striped body; two pairs of wings and narrow waist; only females sting
Diet: adults eat nectar, fruit juice, and tree **sap**; larvae eat insects

FACT

Female wasps have to fight to become the next queen. Fights can last for several days. The queen is the only wasp that can lay eggs in the nest. Her eggs hatch into female workers. There may be 6,000 workers in a nest.

Narrow waist

Head

Striped abdomen

Wing

Paper Walls

Wasps make their nests out of paper! They collect wood fibers and chew them up to make a paste. They mold the paste into six-sided chambers. It then dries solid.

27

STINK BU

*T*hese bugs really do stink! When they are attacked, the bugs release a powerful smell. The smell is too much for birds, lizards, and other **predators**.

Stink bugs eat liquid food, which they suck through a tube-shaped mouth. Most stink bugs drink the sap of smelly plants, such as cabbage. They store the smelly chemicals in the sap inside the thorax. When a predator comes too close, the bug raises its abdomen and squirts out the smelly liquid from holes on its belly. Adult bugs can fly away from trouble. Baby bugs, or nymphs, have no wings, so the spray is their best defense.

Back wings

Head

Wing case

Armored thorax

UP CLOSE

Some stink bugs are meat eaters. They munch on ladybugs and caterpillars. They also eat poisonous prey that would make birds or mammals sick, but are harmless to stink bugs.

Common name: stink bugs, or shield bugs
Scientific name: Hemiptera
Length: 0.2 in (5 mm) to 1 in (2.5 cm)
Key features: oval body is flat at the top; adults have two pairs of wings
Diet: most suck sap from plants; a few bugs prey on smaller insects, especially soft larvae

Mating Calls

Some stink bugs try to impress mates with a song. The bug scrapes a row of pegs on its leg against ridges on its tummy. It is a bit like playing a violin!

GLOSSARY

abdomen The rearmost part of an insect's body, behind the thorax.

antenna (antennae) A long, thin stalk on a bug's head, used for detecting movements, odors, and tastes.

dung The waste material left over from food pushed out of the body.

female The animal sex that produces young as eggs or babies.

foam A bubbling liquid, sometimes made by an animal.

grub A baby beetle.

host The animal upon which a parasite lives and feeds.

insect An animal with six legs and a body divided into three sections.

invertebrate An animal without a backbone (spine) or other bones.

larva (larvae) The young stage in the life cycle of a bug, when it hatches out of its eggs.

maggot The young stage of a bug, usually a fly, when it has hatched but has not yet become an adult.

male The animal sex that does not produce young.

mammal A warm-blooded animal that feeds its babies with milk and has fur or hair.

nectar A sugary liquid made by flowers to attract insects.

nymph A stage in the life cycle of some bugs; nymphs look like small adults without wings.

pollen A yellow dust made by flowers so they can reproduce.

predator An animal that hunts other animals for food.

prey An animal that is hunted by another animal for food.

sap A liquid made by plants or trees.

social Living in large groups.

stinger Part of an animal that can deliver a sting.

thorax The middle section of an insect's body, between the head and abdomen. The six legs are attached to the thorax.

FURTHER RESOURCES

Books about bugs

Llewellyn, Claire. *The Best Book of Bugs.* New York: Kingfisher, 2005.

Mitchell, Susan K. *Biggest Vs. Smallest Creeply, Crawly Creatures.* Berkeley Heights, NJ: Enslow Elementary, 2010.

Parker, Steve. *Extreme Bugs: Creepy and Crawly, Mad and Bad!* Hauppage, NY: Barron Educational Series, Inc., 2010.

Winner, Cherie. *Everything Bug: What Kids Really Want to Know About Bugs.* Lanham, MD: NorthWord Press, 2004.

Useful Web sites

Going Bug-gy! Facts and Fun About Insects

http://teacher.scholastic.com/activities/bugs/

National Geographic: Bugs

http://animals.nationalgeographic.com/animals/bugs

INDEX